AF431539

THE POWER OF LETTING GO

7 steps to letting go of the past, learning to forgive and living life to the full

Daniel J. Martin

ISBN 978-9916-746-54-7

Note: This book was created with the intention of offering information, suggestions and guidance on different areas of life, including emotional wellbeing, mental health, personal growth and the development of healthy relationships. However, it is in no way a substitute for professional medical attention or counseling from a qualified psychologist or therapist. If you are dealing with serious emotional or mental health issues, we recommend that you seek professional help immediately.

"Man cannot discover new oceans unless he has the courage to lose sight of the shore."

– Andre Gide

CONTENTS

DOWNLOAD THE AUDIOBOOK FREE!

If you would rather enjoy this book while you drive, walk or work out... **Download the audio version totally FREE!**

Introduction

I'm glad you're holding this book in your hands and I'm even gladder that you've decided to give "letting go" a chance. In the psychology field, this may sound a little abstract or complicated (I promise you that it's not).

Over the following pages, I'll explain what it means to emotionally let go, when it's necessary, and how to do it. Through years of experience, I've discovered that letting go is a process with seven consecutive steps. We'll go through them one by one so you can understand why each one is important.

Before we start, there are two basic ideas you need to keep in mind: first, life is change. Second, life is connection.

Let me explain.

From birth to death, we're constantly changing: we embrace new things and leave others behind. We do this when we stop crawling because we've learned to walk, when we start a new romantic relationship and have to let go of past ones, and when we become independent from our parents. It's natural. Life is about evolving, about moving forward.

On the other hand, throughout this life of change, we form bonds and get emotionally involved with things around us, whether they're people, places, experiences or lessons. These bonds are part of being human and are necessary for our development.

However, some of those bonds become unhealthy over time, leading to dysfunctional attachments. Instead of helping us grow, they chain us down and drain our energy.

Why don't we just let go of these bonds, just like we stopped crawling or believing in Santa Claus? Well, because we don't always recognize them as toxic, nor do we know how to cut those ties in the right ways.

When bonds become emotional burdens, we often try to ignore them or assume that the pain they cause is normal. We hope that time will heal all wounds, but that's not always the case: time does NOT heal all wounds. What heals is the conscious and voluntary act of letting go of what's hurting you.

What do we mean by "letting go"?

In psychology, letting go means facilitating departure; giving ourselves permission to move on without something we've been carrying, and accepting the consequences that may arise from that separation.

Letting go means no longer clinging to relationships, beliefs, feelings of guilt, resentment, jobs, and so on. It means accepting the change and uncertainty that comes with the new and unknown, and trusting that you are prepared for it.

Letting go also means facing the possible void or feeling of helplessness that follows any separation. That's why it's important to do it right; otherwise, you may find that you relapse and end up chained to new emotional burdens that prevent you from growing or reaching your full potential.

The devil you know...is the devil. Period.

Our ability to adapt is extraordinary (much more than you think!), but we tend to repress it because, when choosing between the devil we know and the unknown good, we often choose the former. This book is about learning to choose the latter, to free yourself from what limits you. If something has been a significant part of your life for a long time, it's not enough to just let it go; a transition period is necessary.

So, this book is for you if:

- You often feel melancholy or nostalgic[1].

---

[1] Melancholy and nostalgia are similar feelings, but they're not the same: while nostalgia is the longing for something specific, melancholy is a vaguer emotion that's not always linked to something concrete.

- You've been living on "autopilot" for a while.

- You haven't overcome past traumas.

- You don't feel in control of your life.

- You're afraid of the future or of growing old.

- You feel resentment and bitterness.

- You've been going through a "midlife crisis" for years.

- You think everything was simpler before.

- You have intrusive thoughts about past episodes, both positive and negative, and recurring flashbacks.

- You insist on maintaining your life with as few changes as possible (whether it's your job, your diet, your home décor, your hairstyle, and so on).

Whatever your current situation, your past, or your outlook on life, you have two choices right now: to keep clinging to what's stopping you from growing but giving you a sense of control, or to try letting go and looking back at your chains from a new and liberating perspective.

You may be afraid of taking off and crashing again, just as you have before. You may be terrified of letting go of something and then regretting it. That's normal; I've had those fears too. But you know what? They're part of life. And the only thing that isn't part of life is not moving forward.

Not only is letting go beneficial for your mental health; it's essential for your fulfillment as a human being. Just as you no longer believe in the tooth fairy, but you know that belief was a part of your life (and you're not ashamed of it!), you must let go of other things without feeling insecure or guilty.

If you want to become the best version of yourself—and I assure you that that version is amazing—you need to remove things from your life. You need to do some emotional cleaning up. But it has to be done right. For now, the only thing I ask is that you read this book with an open mind. This way, change will start almost unconsciously. Little by little, you'll progress until you take flight. You'll feel lighter, freer, and more at ease with yourself. You won't forget the past, whether it was happy or painful, but you won't bear the cross of it any more. You'll be able to set sail for the future as a new and renewed person.

And don't worry about what you're leaving behind: you'll keep the valuable and lose only the suffering.

Get ready for a life that starts now. I'm here to help you take off.

Daniel J. Martin

What are you holding onto?

"To fill your cup, you must first empty it."
— Traditional Zen proverb

In the introduction, I mentioned that humans naturally and inevitably form emotional bonds with our surroundings.

These bonds can vary greatly in duration and intensity: some are permanent, like those we have with our children, parents, or the place we were born (though not always). Others are temporary and leave barely a trace after a few years.

To understand how we emotionally engage with our surroundings, it's important to understand what attachment really is.

Attachment and our first bonds

We define attachment as the emotional ties we establish with key people in our lives, those who provide security, love, and a sense of belonging in our early years. Naturally or instinctively, a baby's first attachment figure is their mother[2]. Then come other family members and people who weave the threads of their emotional fabric.

These early attachments influence how you connect with the world today. If those bonds are appropriate, functional, and secure, you are more likely to engage with our environment healthily (without becoming chained to it). If those early attachments are insecure or insufficient, you may encounter more difficulties in maintaining healthy relationships with your surroundings.

---

[2] I'm not saying this is necessarily the case, just that that's the natural predisposition.

The bad news is that those early attachments don't always go the way they should. For various reasons, many of us reach adulthood with emotional deficiencies that push us to form dysfunctional bonds, ranging from dependency to avoidance and isolation.

The good news is that the way you bond (and subsequently un-bond) can be relearned, modified, and healed. An insecure attachment in childhood affects you but it does not determine or doom you. This means that you have the final word, even if you aren't always aware of it.

From a bond to a ball and chain

What do we typically bond with, besides our children and parents? We bond with a profession, friends, partners, other family members, hobbies, a sports team, a culture, a celebrity, a city, a political party, certain habits, activities, interests, and more. All these give us a sense of identity and belonging and help us develop as individuals. However, you must remember that life is change, and all bonds are temporary: you always have the option to break them, and you should do so when they make you suffer or prevent you from moving forward.

Below are the main bonds most of us form throughout our lives:

- Personal relationships, especially romantic ones.

- Family relationships,

- Life stages (childhood, youth, college years, the birth of our first child, and more).

- Places of work or residence.

- Beliefs and social groups.

- Personal achievements (professional, personal, etc.).

- Habits and behaviors.

- Our past.

- Objects and material possessions (a car, a house, a guitar, a boat, a collection, photos, and similar).

- Activities (sports, hobbies, etc.).

- Our body.

Which of the above can become an emotional burden or shackle? Any of them. Any experience that leads you to form a significant bond can potentially turn against you.

Living in the past

Growing up is a natural process that involves letting go of things you're used to when they become obsolete. Most of us do this daily without realizing it. We've already talked about naturally leaving the crawling stage behind. However, when a part of your past filled your life with special meaning, the urge to cling to it can be very strong indeed.

This is what happens to some movie or music stars who once had the world at their feet. After their prime has passed, younger stars come to take their place, as is the natural course of things. Some then insist on competing in areas that are no longer their own, trying to win over an audience that has moved on. They end up devoting their lives to futilely fighting the passage of time, stuck in childish [3] and destructive attitudes, insisting on living in the past.

A similar thing happens with so-called empty nest syndrome: many women who dedicate the best years of their lives to raising children experience a huge void when their children become independent. Often, these women don't understand that the emptiness they feel *is healthy. It's normal*; it's the result of a job well done, with love and commitment. So what's the problem? Well, many of these women see that void as an enemy to be avoided at all costs. If their environment doesn't support them and instead pressures them, making them feel weak or incapable for feeling sad, they start doubting their ability to move forward. This leads to a denial of the new reality and becoming trapped in

---

[3] I'm not defending ageism. It's not that you necessarily need to be young in order to be a star, or that you can't fulfil your dreams or continue your career beyond a certain age. I'm just saying you can't live off the past forever.

limbo between the past that is gone and the present that is not acceptable to them.

You probably know similar cases: that college friend who still reminisces about the good old days and lives for annual reunions; the ex-boyfriend who jumps from relationship to relationship because he's terrified of commitment; the cousin who spends all her savings on cosmetic procedures to look younger, and so on.

In all these cases, the fear of letting go of the past leads to living between two realities: the future, which is rejected, and the past, which will never return.

What are you still holding onto?

I think it's time for you to discover which bonds and attachments aren't working in your life. Figuring them out is usually pretty easy: they're the ones that cause you sadness, anxiety, shame, guilt, a thirst for justice, anger, feelings of inadequacy, low self-esteem, and so on. Many of them relate to past wounds that haven't healed properly. Others are very recent attachments that have created a strong dependence, like a drug.

I invite you to make a list of bonds that you don't feel are healthy or that you experience as burdens—bonds that have become a ball and chain. Don't worry about making a "definitive" list: this is just an initial, provisional one, as it will change over time (it might surprise you!).

Here's an example list based on testimonies from my clients. From experience, I know that the bonds that cause the most pain are, paradoxically, the ones we camouflage the most and that create the strongest emotional dependence. Here's what some of my clients say when I ask what they're holding on to:

- The memory of what happened in my first year of high school / in my childhood / last summer / during my divorce.

- My current relationship with my boss / father / brother / partner.

- The regret of having made or not made that decision.

- The sorrow I feel when I compare my real life with my expectations from my youth.

- My dependence on this habit / addiction / job / person.

- Speculative thoughts (the answers that never came, imagining what might have been, etc.).

- Negative emotions related to my body and the passing of time.

- That decision I know I need to make but can't.

When creating your list, pay attention to how you express these bonds: remember that what keeps you chained to something (for example, a past event) isn't the event itself, but your relationship with it through emotions, obsessive thoughts, rumination, feelings of humiliation, helplessness, fear, and so on. The chains are always emotional, so you need to find the emotion or thought that ties you to each thing: if you haven't gotten over a partner's infidelity, what hurts you isn't the infidelity (after all, it's not happening right now), but YOUR emotions and thoughts related to it.

Once you have that initial list, move on to the next chapter: our step 2 in the process.

Summary of Chapter 1

- Humans naturally and inevitably form bonds.

- These bonds can be with places, people, memories, stages of our lives, and even traumas.

- Some of these bonds and attachments become toxic over time or prevent us from moving forward, even if we don't realize it.

- Toxic bonds are those that cause us distress, sadness, feelings of inadequacy, anger, shame, and more, but we don't know how to let them go.

Why you need to let go

*"If you can't do anything about it then let it go.
Don't be a prisoner to things you can't change."*

— Tony Gaskins

We've already talked about how it's impossible not to form bonds with the things in life. The goal isn't to avoid bonding, but to recognize what needs to be let go of when the time comes. Sounds easy, right? So why is it so hard to cut the ties that bind us?

There are several reasons. Here are the main ones:

1. We don't always recognize these bonds as unhealthy. Often, we're not aware of how attached we are to something (a person, a

memory, a place) because we're so used to it. We don't realize that it's not a healthy attachment but rather a dependency or addiction. This applies to a relationship post-breakup with an ex we don't want to let go of, or a relationship with alcohol.

2. Unhealthy or obsolete attachments are "trained" not to bother us too much. We kid ourselves with excuses like: "This is just how it's always been," "It's my family, I can't do anything about it," "If I change this, I'll lose that and I can't afford to," "If I had a different personality, I'd do it, but I'm just like this…". We end up assuming that it's normal to bear emotional burdens that harm us because they're "part of who we are".

3. Many things we cling to now were positive in the past, so we don't see them as harmful. We've already mentioned how those happy and fruitful college years can paradoxically become shackles, leading someone to continue an inappropriate lifestyle for decades, turning them into someone pathetic and immature.

4. We're aware of the harm a bond is causing, but we don't know how to make the change. We don't know how to leave that thing behind.

5. The most frequent and uncomfortable reason: fear. Fear of consequences, the void, even greater pain, loneliness, or failure in the future. So, we cling to the shadow of what once was in order to deny the desolation of its absence.

Why can't we let go of a painful past?

All living things feel safer with the known than with the new. Only when we can clearly see the advantages of living without something, or when we are forced by a greater power, can we abandon it. Otherwise, as we've said, our brain prefers the devil it knows over the angel it doesn't. This is part of our survival instinct (subconsciously thinking: "If we've survived this way so far, why risk changing?"). This makes sense if the past is positive, but what about when it's traumatic?

Many clients ask me why, if they're aware of the harm of mentally reliving a traumatic event, they can't stop doing it. It's very common: stressful or overwhelming experiences often stay with us in the form of humiliating memories, feelings of guilt, shame, anxiety, fear, and so on. They stick to us and follow us everywhere, shaping our lives and decisions.

Why does this happen? Because, in a way, it's our brain's way of keeping us alert about an experience it couldn't process. The message our nervous system sends is: "Listen, that event was dangerous. My duty is to remind you of it constantly, so you don't let your guard down." It sounds logical, except that the memory provokes emotions that hinder our progress and development.

Take this example: we all have a first time we burned our fingers, usually between the ages of one and five. Whether it's with a candle, a hot pan, or a radiator, that first burn teaches us about fire or high temperatures, and our brain records it to prevent that painful experience from happening again. Keeping us away from pain is part of its mission, so, from then on, it'll remind us of the burn every time we get close to a candle, bonfire or stove.

Now, imagine your brain is so impacted by that first burn that it keeps obsessing over it. Instead of understanding it as an experience to learn from ("be careful with fire"), it can't process it, can't find an explanation, and starts influencing your decisions chaotically, even when they have nothing to do with fire: your brain reminds you of that burn all the time; it causes anxiety attacks even when there's no fire around; it distracts you at work; it gives you nightmares, insomnia, addictions, mental blocks and more. It doesn't realize that you're no longer that child who didn't know the dangers of fire and tries to protect you until it ends up harming you by not allowing you to live a normal life and grow because it's too stuck trying to protect you from fire.

That's what happens with traumatic events. Your brain can't find a way to deal with them and constantly reminds you in order to protect you. However, this only makes you suffer needlessly. The more you suffer, the more the brain insists on keeping you alert, since clearly, you haven't "overcome" it yet. This becomes a vicious cycle.

The decision you don't want to make

You might be thinking: "Well, if it's so hard to let go of a bond, there must be a reason. Maybe what we're clinging to still serves a purpose in our lives, right? Why mess with it?"

That's a good question. The answer is that holding on instead of letting go limits your potential and keeps you from being the best version of yourself: the version where you're happy and living the life you want.

Trauma shouldn't stay with you as an open wound just for "protection". While you may never forget some of the things you've been through, you can change how you relate to the past.

Because the past is a place to learn from, not a place to live in.

Why we should let go

Here's an example of why it's necessary to let go: imagine someone you know has an accident and breaks their leg. After a period in a cast, they start the recovery phase with crutches, as instructed by doctors.

Now imagine that, years later, you meet this person again, and they're still walking with crutches. What would you think? Possibly that their leg didn't heal properly. But what if you knew their leg had been ready to walk without crutches for a long time? I'm guessing you'd encourage them to leave the crutches behind. And what if they told you they were afraid of falling again? Or that they were so used to the crutches they would never give them up? You'd probably point out all the things they were missing out on by using crutches: playing sports, dancing with their partner, picking up their children, playing with their dog... Would it seem logical to you that this person would give up all that out of fear?

The bonds we don't want to let go of are like crutches: they made sense in the past but are no longer useful in the present. The fear of letting go limits us and chains us to a safety zone we no longer need.

A dignified life

If someone asked me for one reason to break free from emotional chains, my answer would be this:

the incompatibility between being a slave and living a dignified life.

When a human is enslaved, they don't just lose their physical freedom: their dignity as a person is taken away, meaning they're no longer recognized as someone with rights and will, someone who owns their own destiny.

Similarly, emotional chains, traumatic bonds, dependency and the like take away our dignity by limiting our freedom and will.

Besides this essential moral reason, there are many more reasons why it's worth breaking free from the chains. What are those reasons? The same ones you'd give to someone using crutches they don't need, which have to do with reaching our full potential.

What happens when we let go?

When you let go of a burden, and I mean truly let go, meaning you're no longer emotionally tied to something, the void fills with good things. Trust me, I've experienced it. When you genuinely let go, here's what happens:

- You feel liberated, like a weight has been lifted off your shoulders.

- You regain self-confidence.

- You recover your self-esteem and sense of dignity.

- Anger diminishes. You stop fighting with the world and dwelling on injustice.

- You become more tolerant of what happens in the present, especially minor incidents.

- Your personal relationships become more sincere and enriching. You're not afraid to give (love, kindness and so on) or receive (love, support, companionship and more).

- Your energy and vitality improve. It's true: mind and body are one, and if the mind is less burdened, so is the body.

- The decisions you make lead to better outcomes because they're not influenced by distorted filters.

- You can break through your own limitations.

- You feel proud of yourself.

- Your opportunities improve, and you earn more money (I promise, it's true!).

- You act more and complain less.

- You laugh more, alone or with others. Your sense of humor improves. You live with more joy.

- You let others be themselves without feeling threatened by their freedom.

Living without crutches

Now, let's focus on you: what are you missing out on by using crutches?

I invite you to revisit your list of bonds from the previous chapter and think of those attachments as the crutches you use to walk. Next, consider what you're missing out on by using those crutches.

Ask yourself these questions for each of them:

1. What was this bond/crutch like in the past or at the beginning of the bond?

2. Does it still provide what it did back then? If so, why do I think it makes me feel so bad now?

3. What would I gain by cutting this tie?

4. What consequences would I have to face right now? Would it be worth it?

5. If I'm afraid to cut ties suddenly, is there a way to take gradual steps? Do I have any support?

6. If there were no negative consequences for anyone, would I cut this bond right now?

The answers to these questions will give you the strength and conviction you need to start letting go.

Your future objectives

A reasonable fear of letting go of the past is often reinforced if you're not clear about your future goals, excited about what's coming, or motivated to improve. Then, letting go seems less meaningful than holding onto negative attachments. Because why give up the crutches if you don't have goals that involve using your legs?

That's why it's important to make an effort to find your purposes and goals in life. This book isn't about finding life goals, but it's necessary to see that there's an exciting path ahead in order to stop looking back[4].

Personal goals can vary greatly from person to person. You just need to be clear about what yours are and what's realistically keeping you from them. Remember, a goal is not just a wish; it's an intention to act. Because things don't change by themselves.

I have goals and a purpose, but still nothing changes in my life

---

[4] If you want to go into depth on your goals and purposes, I recommend "The Power of Goals" from this series: *www.danieljmartin.es/po*

Some clients tell me that despite being clear about their future projects and goals, nothing changes.

This happens because the brain can't find any recompense in hypothetical future benefits and resists letting go, just in case. In most cases, it turns out those projects or goals aren't really my clients'. Whose are they? Who knows! Often, we adopt goals that are simply what others expect of us. We do what our parents expect, act as society wants, and don't question much more beyond that. This might not be so bad if it weren't for the fact that what others expect often serves them more than it does us.

If you can't let go of the past despite thinking you're clear about what you want for the next few years, make sure your desires are truly yours. From experience, I know it's likely that your goals (especially the legitimate goal of being happy) won't please someone close to you. And it's possible that several people around you won't be thrilled with so much "freedom" on your part. It's sad but true.

So it wouldn't hurt to ask yourself who would genuinely be happy to see you live in peace and freedom and who would see it as a problem or threat. Because the harsh reality is that sometimes we give up being who we want to be to obtain certain people's love or approval. Then, we choose goals that are "kind" to everyone instead of finding what would truly make us happy. We stick with plan B in order to avoid feeling alone with plan A.

In terms of the fear of failure, I'll tell you one thing: the only real failure is not trying at all.

Summary of Chapter 2

- The main reason we don't let go is fear.

- Our nervous system clings to past traumatic experiences so we don't forget them. It's only trying to protect us from suffering them again.

- Letting go of what hurts us is an act of self-love.

- Emotional chains, like slavery, condemn us to an undignified life where we're not in control.

- When we let go, we give ourselves the opportunity to receive good things.

Going back to the beginning

"The cave you fear to enter holds the treasure you seek."

— Joseph Campbell

So far, we've talked about what bonds are and why we form them. I've asked you to make a list of your dysfunctional bonds and to think about what you're giving up by holding on to them. We've also discussed the need to let go of emotional crutches as a step toward the future life you desire and deserve.

Now, it's time to travel into the past.

This chapter may be the most painful of the book: you'll need to delve into your emotional archives to find the origin of all those attachments, limitations, and habits that are now hurting you but that you can't seem to let go of.

In some cases, the journey to the beginning is short and straightforward. For example, maybe you can't speak in public because once, as a child, someone laughed at you when you tried, and your brain has kept you away from that pain ever since.

In other cases, you'll **need to rewrite the story.**

Rewrite the story? Can you change the past now?

No, you can't change the past. But you can change the way you understand it. I'm not talking about falsifying what happened, deceiving yourself, sugarcoating anything, or making excuses. I'm talking about giving it an ending, since that traumatic past still lives in the present, even though the event ended long ago. You need to give the story an ending in the present to be able to let it go.

Before we proceed, consider two things:

- First, you need to **accept your past right now**.

- Second, you need to be **willing to change your thoughts about it**.

Accepting the past once and for all

We've already said that the past can't be changed. Therefore, we must make the effort to accept it as it is, understanding that "accepting" doesn't mean we like it, agree with it, or have "given up". Accepting simply means acknowledging that it happened that way.

I'll give you an example: in the fourteenth century, a plague epidemic killed a third of the world's population. Across Europe, Africa, and Asia, the Black Death killed about eighty million people in a few years, leaving many towns and cities with no living inhabitants. This is a proven fact, and as such, we accept it, no matter how horrible it is. We accept it as fact, even if we don't like it. In the same way, we must accept:

1. That such a traumatic event in our life occurred, no matter how much it displeases us or how unfair it was.

2. That the event isn't happening right now, meaning it ended physically. It's no longer in our home, nor part of our day. It didn't just happen right now. It's not happening while you read these lines. It's in the past.

3. That the best way to accept it is to learn from it.

For many people, this third point is the hardest, because there isn't always an evident lesson to compensate for the pain. If you go back to the burn example, it's easy to deduce a lesson: in this case, it's not to put your fingers near the fire. But what about traumatic experiences that you didn't choose? What lesson do you learn from a father who never loved you? Or from suffering in adolescence because you weren't attractive enough? Or from being a victim of bullying? Shouldn't others be the ones to learn from their actions?

Yes, definitely, but you can't control what others do. Your learning in these cases must be about what happened to you as a result of that event. About how the specific event turned into trauma and why. About your strengths and your way of being. The learning must be self-knowledge.

Why? Because in these cases, what lies behind the trauma is your primitive brain (the part that only thinks about keeping you away from danger) trying to protect you.

Keys to accepting the past

Here are some reflections and ideas that can help you make peace with your past. I invite you to read the sentences several times and consider how much you agree with them. The goal is to assimilate them and keep those that are most helpful to you:

- My past does not define me.

- The abuse and injustices I suffered in the past aren't my fault, even if I allowed them by action or omission.

- I've suffered enough because of this. Now, it's time to grow.

- Mistakes and life's blows are part of the human experience. We all have them.

- I want to see my past mistakes and bad decisions as opportunities to learn.

- I forgive myself for past actions and decisions that hurt me and/or others and commit to learning from them.

- I forgive myself for staying where I never should have stayed: I probably didn't understand what was happening.

- I forgive myself for not stopping something when I should have: I probably wasn't ready yet.

- I forgive myself for hurting myself in the past as punishment for not achieving success, love, or approval.

- Everyone has a past, and everyone has parts of their past that cause pain. Instead of blaming myself, I commit to seeing the experience as a way to learn more about myself and my strengths.

The reason we do the things we do

Everything that keeps you tied to something or someone has a reason for being. Even bad habits, toxic relationships, and seemingly simple decisions that you never wanted to make have a reason: behind them is your most primitive and instinctive brain protecting you from something repeating itself (or at least trying to).

The ultimate mission of your brain and nervous system is to keep you alive. To do so, it doesn't hesitate to keep you away from anything that represents a potential threat, even if that means clinging to something that in the past gave you some sense of security or affection (or so you perceived), but now prevents you from growing.

If you suffer because of it, your nervous system is aware but can't find alternatives. You must be the one to provide those options. And to do that, you need to seek answers.

Now, it's time to figure out where everything went wrong, that is, at what point you clung to something because an emotional need of yours turned against you.

The healing journey

The vast majority of emotional traumas can be understood as an attack or threat to one of these two basic human needs (or sometimes both):

- Our need for love (security, affection, protection, care, acceptance and so on).

- Our need for physical and moral integrity (including our dignity as people, our identity, recognition of our existence as independent beings, and so on).

Now, I'd like you to think of an event from your past that has followed you into the present as a trauma. If this is too painful for you, please choose a less significant incident: something that simply annoyed you and that you still think about occasionally.

Take about thirty minutes to make this journey, preferably at the end of your day (but not right before sleeping).

1. Sit in front of a mirror and look at yourself while you remember.

2. Now, explain to yourself what happened as if you didn't already know. Explain it as if the person listening (you, in the mirror) knows nothing about what happened but cares about how you feel.

3. Allow yourself to feel all the emotions that arise.

4. When you finish telling yourself about the event, ask yourself what worries you about it right now. What harm can the event cause you right now? (I'm not talking about the limitations

it caused you. I'm asking what it can do to you right now, in this room, or this week).

5. Take a deep breath and do the exercise again. Tell yourself the event again as if you didn't know it. Try to do it the same way as before, though you might remember new details or focus on it slightly differently.

6. When you've told yourself the story again, ask yourself again what worries you about it right now and how it can harm you now.

7. Repeat this two or three more times. You should end up mentally exhausted and bored with this exercise. Ideally, you'll feel this is overwhelming and need a break because you don't want to keep talking about it.

If you do this exercise over several sessions, your emotions will change. The person listening to you in the mirror (you) will show you the compassion and love you haven't had for yourself regarding this. You'll feel less fear and more connected to yourself and the person you were then. You'll feel that the event no longer terrifies you as much. Your anxiety will decrease.

When you have had some practice, try writing down how you feel after each session of repeating the same story to yourself. You'll be pleasantly surprised.

The ego in wounds of the past

Therapist Meredith Miller says that the wounds we carry from the past give us a false sense of identity and familiarity, which is why it's so hard to let them go. We feel that the wounds give meaning to part of our existence, when in reality it's the opposite: we try to adapt our existence to them to avoid more pain.

It's said that most of us carry five primary [5] wounds:

- The wound of abandonment.

- The wound of betrayal.

- The wound of humiliation.

- The wound of injustice.

- The wound of rejection.

I've been in this profession for many years and I've yet to meet anyone who doesn't carry at least one of these five wounds from childhood. Most people carry at least three of them traumatically.

These five wounds can and should be healed. But if you haven't done so, the problem is that,

---

[5] It was Canadian therapist Lise Bourbeau who first proposed these five categories for all the traumas of being human. They are covered in her book *Heal Your Wounds and Find Your True Self*.

without intending to, you expose ourself to having these wounds repeat and deepen. Why? Because you repeat the patterns. Because, for your false ego (the most superficial one), these wounds are your identity. And because, unfortunately, abusive and toxic people will come to attack you right where the wound is.

As Meredith Miller points out, all other blows that come your way in life will fall on those untreated wounds. Your nervous system will accumulate emotional wound upon emotional wound without having time to heal.

That's why it's essential to travel to the past to embrace and understand these five wounds.

Traveling to the first time

How can you repair this? There are various proposals from the fields of psychology and psychiatry.

For example, motivational author John Purkiss explains a technique for repairing the past in his book *The Power of Letting Go*. It's similar to telling yourself the story in front of the mirror: again, you go to your emotional archive, but in this case, to find the first time you felt each wound.

Although it's uncomfortable or painful, he suggests mentally recalling the first time you felt humiliated, mistreated, unjustly accused, abandoned, misunderstood, and so on. That first time probably happened in your childhood, even though you didn't know what it was about or how it would affect you in the future.

Back in the present, Purkiss proposes being attentive to the negative emotions of your daily life. For example, if you have a disagreement with your neighbor and become excessively angry because they disrespected you. Or your partner makes a comment that disappoints you and completely destabilizes you. Or you still feel resentment for that time your brother let you down. Now, go to your archive of emotions and find the first time you felt that way.

When you find the event that caused the first wound (it might be very painful, or it might be a trivial childhood thing), indulge and allow yourself to feel all the emotions. You might feel indignation, pain, and frustration that you repressed the first time to avoid bigger problems. You might also feel a lot of shame for having those feelings. Today, you're no longer that ashamed or insecure child: allow yourself to feel whatever you want about that memory. Remember, while not all behaviors are acceptable or valid, all emotions are.

What we're doing with this exercise of finding the first time is, in Purkiss' words: "We look inward, find the original incident that caused the discomfort, and complete it. We complete the experience by reliving it from beginning to end. We relive to repair."

If you repeat these exercises often and with increasingly overwhelming events, you'll soon feel stronger and more at peace with yourself.

Why does this happen?

Because we tend to repress emotions to forget, and that doesn't work. It's like trying to keep a soccer ball submerged underwater by holding it down with your hands: it takes tremendous effort, and whenever it slips, it pops to the surface with force and hits you in the face. Instead, if you let it slowly rise to the surface, guiding it with your hands, and allow it to float on the surface, it won't bother you after a while. You can't eliminate the ball, but now it doesn't disturb you: there's plenty of pool to swim in, and the ball takes up very little space.

Summary of Chapter 3

- We must accept our past, understanding that "accepting" doesn't mean we like it.

- Accepting the past also means understanding that it's over and isn't with us in our daily lives, whether it was good or bad.

- The past doesn't define or condemn us.

- The past is a place to learn from, not a place to live in.

- We must travel to the past to repair it, allowing ourselves to understand and embrace all the emotions, thoughts, and actions it forced us to have at that time.

- We all have at least one of these five soul wounds that we resist letting go of: the wound of abandonment, the wound of betrayal, the wound of humiliation, the wound of injustice, and the wound of rejection.

Control your thoughts

"You realize that our mistrust of the future makes it hard to give up the past."

— Chuck Palahniuk

In this chapter, we're going to work on changing the thoughts that keep us attached to dysfunctional bonds.

First, let me congratulate you on the effort you made in the previous chapter. Facing a painful past is something only brave and committed people do. Don't worry if you're still in the process of acceptance or if there are days when it feels like you're going backward: the important thing is your will and commitment to the future.

Now, we're going to talk about everything we tell ourselves to convince ourselves of something: all the excuses, distorted thoughts, erroneous beliefs, and lies we tell ourselves to justify holding on to something.

How can you convince your brain to do an "emotional cleanup"? How do you break its resistance?

Our survival and protection instinct gets stressed with every new change, but it calms down if it sees that we're prepared for it. Going back to the example of the first burn, today we can be close to a lit candle without having a panic attack: we know what happened, we know how it hurt back then, but we've let go of all the suffocating and paralyzing emotions related to that burn. We no longer suffer every day because of that time we got burned, and we can continue with our life and growth.

Next, we'll see why it's so important to manage our own thoughts.

The emotions-thoughts-actions triangle

Your nervous system, led by the brain, is responsible for developing your responses to external stimuli. The brain generates emotions, thoughts, and actions. These three elements form a feedback loop:

- **Thoughts:** These are the mental processes and conclusions from all the information we receive from the outside, which our brain interprets, organizes, stores, and retrieves for later use. This includes habits, judgments, beliefs, learning, memories, ideas, and so on.

- **Emotions:** These are the subjective responses and affective reactions we experience in relation to stimuli and their mental interpretation: love, sadness, anger, disgust, surprise, happiness, joy, and similar.

- **Actions:** These are our voluntary behaviors, the actions we consciously and observably perform in response to our emotions and thoughts. Actions can include both verbal and non-verbal behaviors and are also considered a form of communication and expression.

These three elements influence and condition each other. You can't control the events that trigger your emotions, nor the emotions themselves, but you can control how you understand and react to them from a cognitive standpoint (thoughts). If you control your thoughts, you control your emotions and actions. If you control all of that, you'll be able to let go with tranquility and confidence.

Combat pessimistic anticipation

The resistance to letting go hides a fear of what will happen next. When you consider a future without what has been with you for so long (without those crutches), anxiety triggers a bunch of "What if this happens?", "What if that happens?", "What if I regret it?"—always with terrible assumptions, most of which never happen.

That's why you need to train our mind to respond effectively to anticipatory anxiety and catastrophic thoughts.

Here's an exercise for you:

1. Find a quiet place where you can reflect for a while without interruptions and think about what your life would be like without the thing you don't want to let go of.

2. Make a mental list of all the terrible things that could happen if you let go of that thing/person/habit. Think of the worst-case

scenarios, the ones that would hurt you the most, the most catastrophic things you can imagine.

3. Familiarize yourself with their consequences. Indulge in the worst possible outcomes, even if they're exaggerated: your family abandons you, you end up living on charity, you go to jail...the worst of the worst. Embrace the anxiety this produces.

4. Start asking yourself questions to put all these misfortunes in perspective: What would really happen if you got fired? How would you feel? And after a year, how do you think you'd feel? Would you be the only person in the world who has gone through that? How serious is it really what people think of you? Are there really so many possibilities that this misfortune will occur? What can you do here and now to try to avoid that? Is it in your hands? What would make you feel more at ease?

The goal of this exercise is to send a message of calm to your brain by putting the "disasters" in perspective—not because those misfortunes aren't possible but because you'll be able to face them when they appear. The message is: "I don't need to suffer today for something that may never happen. And I shouldn't suffer for futures I can't control either. Taking certain measures now and trusting myself, for now, is enough."

Learn to think better: Mindfulness

I propose another technique for controlling thoughts. You've probably heard of mindfulness. Mindfulness is a mental training technique whose ultimate goal is to learn to find the best possible response to each present or past circumstance. Over time, this mental training becomes an automatic habit, like the habit of having breakfast, and helps us make decisions and act in the best possible way according to who we are and our values. People who master mindfulness can respond to any life challenge without breaking down or losing control, and can be at peace with their past.

How is this achieved?

Mindfulness uses meditation as its main technique. Meditation involves seeking full attention, focusing the mind on one point or idea (such as your breathing, ambient sound, a specific visualization, a body part and so on) during training sessions, and not allowing that attention to drift elsewhere. The idea is to learn to voluntarily silence all the mental noise, the carousel of intrusive and automatic thoughts, emotional pain, impulsivity, anxiety, and confusion we carry with you. It's learning to put your brain on pause.

Once the brain is trained, you can transfer that control exercise to your daily reality. That's when you're able to maintain the right attitude toward everything that requires a response from you, instead of reacting without thinking or following obsolete behavior patterns that you maintain only because you haven't rationally analyzed them.

With mindfulness, you create a mental and temporal space between the external stimulus, the thought, and your subsequent action. If you get lost in thoughts and emotions, you lose the anchor of the present, which is the only moment in which you can act.

If you want to learn more about this incredible tool, I recommend reading "The Power of Mindfulness" from this same collection:

www.danieljmartin.es/books/pom

In anxiety's defense

Now, I'm going to stand up for your main defense mechanism: anxiety. We can all agree that anxiety is very unpleasant. It puts you in a state of confusion, panic, despair, blockage, incapacity to act, and enormous suffering, as well as giving you feelings of inadequacy.

However, anxiety, at its core, has good intentions: its goal isn't to harm you (even though it does) but to warn you of imminent danger. Why, if its goal is to protect you, is it so counterproductive? Because it conveys the message in a very unpleasant and paralyzing way, often in situations that don't pose a real danger: many people end up in the emergency room due to an anxiety attack, thinking it's a heart attack or a psychotic episode. This happens because their nervous system is altered by previous events and is now hypervigilant. However, the person misinterprets the symptoms and ends up in the hospital thinking they're going to die.

So, what do we do with anxiety? Is it good or bad? Anxiety is just the messenger. You shouldn't ignore it, but you should be able to interpret its warnings instead of frustrating and exhausting yourself with the symptoms it causes.

If you deal with daily anxiety spikes, I recommend not feeling guilty or ashamed about it: it means your nervous system is working. Instead of suffering, invest time in understanding that anxiety. Why does it spike? When do you think it started? Does it have to do with a specific wound or event, or a particular stage of your life? What do you think needs to happen for your anxiety to go away?

Anxiety just wants to protect you. Don't ignore it, because it won't go away: it will come back again and again until you can respond to its message.

Accepting the problems of the present

Letting go doesn't mean denying what's there or trying to forget it magically. Letting go isn't forgetting. Also, it's not always as easy as blocking someone on your phone (sometimes it is, but usually, it takes more than that). Letting go often requires more than just slamming a door.

We've done the exercise of accepting the past. Now let's deal with what surrounds us at this very moment:

How do you accept the present if you don't like it?

The exercise I propose now is practiced daily by millions of people, by believers in the form of prayer, and by those who follow the Alcoholics Anonymous program.

This is the version I suggest:

1. Find a quiet place where you can focus on your thoughts for a few minutes without being interrupted.

2. Once you've anchored your mind in the here and now (avoiding letting your brain wander with random thoughts), repeat aloud or mentally the following phrase:

3. *"I will seek serenity to accept the things I cannot change, courage to change the things I can, and wisdom to know the difference."*

If you're a believer, you can ask God for those three things (serenity, courage, and wisdom). If you're not, you can dedicate this prayer to yourself and commit to seeking those three things daily.

Making room for gratitude

The more you take things personally, the more stress you suffer. The more stress you carry, the more exhausted you are and the less capacity you have to fight for your interests and your present and future wellbeing.

However, it sometimes seems like you only take things personally when they're bad. The good things, you don't even notice!

That's why it's important to practice gratitude for the good things you do have. Because, when you spend too much time focused on your problems, you lose sight not only of perspective but of everything around you. You stop giving importance to the things you do have and ignore them because you're too immersed in your problems, both past and future.

At this point, you need to lift our gaze from the ground to look ahead, even at the risk of stumbling and falling. Because you're letting good things pass by without even noticing.

Now, I ask you to make a list of things you can be grateful for today. Here are some examples to get you started.

Things to be grateful for in the present:

- Something related to health.

- Something related to work.

- Something related to those around you (family, partner, friends, etc.).

- Something related to the place you live (e.g., there are no wars or killings).

- Something good that has happened to you this year.

- Something good that has happened to you today.

- Having the ability to love sincerely (not everyone has this).

- Having or having had the love of a partner, mother, father, friends, etc.

- Having the ability to see good things in life.

- Having good friends (many or a few).

- Having the following qualities: (list the ones you consider important and are most proud of).

The exercise in gratitude doesn't end here. Now, I ask you to add a "but" every time you feel sad about something. And that "but" should be one of the things you're grateful for in this life, one of the things on your list. For example: you're sad because you feel you could have gone further in your professional career, BUT your health is good. You get angry every time you remember what they did to you that time, BUT you're grateful to have the intelligence you do. You suffer the humiliation of that partner who betrayed you, BUT you're grateful to count on that friend who supported you.

In "The Power of Gratitude", I delve deeper into the importance of this technique. I also share the gratitude journal I've created exclusively for my clients: *www.danieljmartin.es/books/pogr*

The GLAD technique

This exercise is proposed by Donald Altman[6] to put bad things and emotional wounds into perspective. Again, it's not about downplaying your traumas (in any case, trying to "downplay" them doesn't work). It's about giving importance to the good things that also deserve your attention.

GLAD is an acronym formed by the words "Gratitude," "Learning," "Accomplishment," and "Delight". It's a technique that focuses precisely

---

[6] Donald Altman is a psychotherapist, mindfulness coach, former Buddhist monk and speaker for personal growth. His works include *The Mindfulness Toolbox: 50 Practical Tips, Tools & Handouts for Anxiety, Depression, Stress & Pain.*

on finding, during the exercise, an example for each of these terms.

These examples should be different every day or every time the exercise is done.

What is this exercise for?

If done once, like the other proposed exercises, it won't do much. But if repeated until it becomes training and a habit, the results are spectacular:

- On the one hand, it puts the problems of the past and present into perspective. That way, they don't seem so overwhelming, and you're more capable of letting them go (again, it's not about downplaying problems or traumas; it's about giving yourself more confidence to face them).

- On the other hand, it counteracts the so-called "gravity" that our past exerts on you: if you divert most of your energy to the present (as it should be), the past will take a backseat.

Let's get started with the GLAD exercise:

1. To start, I recommend doing it like the previous exercises, with a brief retreat from reality. Find a secluded and quiet place to think. With practice, you'll be able to do the GLAD exercises on a bus ride, in the shower, while preparing dinner, in a traffic jam, and more.

2. Control your breathing and your thoughts. When you have them under control, visualize, one by one, the four words of the GLAD acronym (Gratitude, Learning, Accomplishment, and Delight), understanding what each one means.

3. Think of an example from your life for each one. Starting with GRATITUDE, you can feel grateful for very general things (good health, a roof over your head, a partner who loves you), or for specific things, like having had a good morning at work today.

4. Do the same with all the words. In the case of LEARNING, it can be anything from a small trick to opening a container to everything you've learned in your career.

5. In the case of ACCOMPLISHMENT, you can interpret this as any success you've had today, this month, or ten years ago; and it can be an individual, collective achievement, or part of a larger personal project.

6. Finally, DELIGHT should come from something you've noticed in your environment, like feeling cheered by a joke or a drawing your child did. It should be something that made you smile spontaneously.

The GLAD exercise will give you confidence in yourself and your environment. It will make you see that you do many things well in your life, reinforce your motivation and commitment, and give you reasons to live with optimism.

Summary of Chapter 4

- To let go of the bonds that chain you, you must convince your brain that we're prepared for it.

- To achieve this, you must change how you think about things, being aware of your erroneous beliefs, pessimistic thoughts, prejudices, and so on.

- Mindfulness is a good way to learn to change your thinking and attitude toward reality.

- You must make an effort to appreciate the good things you have, as they are often buried by problems.

Facing grief

"I must be willing to give up what I am in order to become what I will be."

— Albert Einstein

Grief is the process of adapting to a significant loss or change. We often associate it with the death of a family member, but it can also be due to the loss of a job or a romantic breakup, for example.

Throughout our lives, we will have to face several instances of grief. It is part of our human condition and essence, so the best approach is to meet these instances with maximum mental preparation. What does this mean? First and foremost, it means allowing ourselves to feel the pain for as long as necessary.

What things can we grieve for? In truth, any change in our lives that causes sadness can trigger grief:

- The death of a loved one.

- The end of a phase in our lives.

- A romantic breakup.

- An accident or tragedy.

- A falling out with someone in our circle due to a betrayal or fight.

- The loss of something important: a job, our health, our home...

- Rejection.

- A broken childhood dream.

- A failed or interrupted project.

- An amputation or significant surgery.

- Letting go of something that has accompanied us for a long time: from selling the family home to overcoming a childhood trauma (in this last case, the grief is not for the trauma but for leaving the trauma behind).

Grieving the loss of something or someone valuable is inevitable, whether we are aware of it or not. When it's something obvious, we grieve consciously: we give ourselves recovery time, allow ourselves to cry, and so on. But sometimes, we are unaware that we need to grieve for something. In that case, we conflict with our emotional needs by denying ourselves the chance to mourn the loss or by trying to shorten the transition time to "recover" as soon as possible. Then, the grief can become pathological.

A loss that is not properly assimilated will lead to emotional problems in the future. It's our nervous system demanding the time or attention it didn't receive for grieving, and it will continue to create discomfort until it's completed. On the other hand, well-processed grief not only allows us to continue our lives in peace but also improves our capabilities and resources to deal with future situations of loss, frustration, or suffering.

We must remember that grief is part of life. I don't know anyone who hasn't had to face some form of it.

How long does grief last? Each person faces changes differently, and the same circumstance affects each individual differently. Even so, it is generally considered that "normal" grief lasts one year, coinciding with the anniversary of the event that triggered it and passing through each significant date without that person or habit once.

Stages of the grieving process

The grieving process goes through several phases, which last for more or less time depending on the case until the new situation is accepted.

It was psychiatrist Elisabeth Kübler-Ross, an expert in grief and terminal illness support, who proposed the well-known five stages of grief[7].

The five stages of grief, in order, are:

1. **Denial:** At first, there is disbelief at what has happened. "It can't be," is the first thing we think. "This isn't happening," "It's a mistake," and similar. Here, our rational side understands what has happened, but our emotional side does not. Our real emotions have not yet surfaced.

2. **Anger:** Recognizing what has happened, we enter a phase of anger, rage, and a sense of

---

[7] The five-stage grief model was first presented by Swiss-American psychiatrist Elisabeth Kübler-Ross in her book *On Death and Dying*, 1969.

injustice. We say: "It's not fair!", "Why me?", "I don't deserve this," "Isn't anyone going to do something?". Anger is natural at this stage of grief and must be allowed.

3. **Bargaining:** In this stage, alternatives to what has happened are sought. We "bargain" with reality to cope with what has happened. Here, it is common to fantasize about other scenarios or the idea of changing reality to make it less harsh: "I need to talk to that person one last time," "God, give me a little more time," "If you give them back to me, I promise...", "Maybe if I do this, I'll get...". It is also common to ruminate on what could have been done to prevent the loss or to attempt things out of time.

4. **Depression**: When the real pain finally arises. It is a period of sadness and pessimism different from the impact of the initial moments. Here, the person has less desire to do things and more difficulty in managing their day-to-day life,

feeling excited, or enjoying things they used to enjoy.

5. **<u>Acceptance</u>**: The loss is accepted, and the person is ready to continue without what has been lost. It is understood that loss is part of life. Often, this phase is accompanied by new habits, new people, a change of residence and similar.

What distinguishes healthy grief from pathological grief? Precisely, moving through these phases. Grief becomes pathological when a person gets stuck in one of the phases. In this case, the emotions, thoughts, and actions related to them do not soften over time as expected; instead, they remain the same or intensify.

Grieving the loss of someone who leaves your life

Just as with literal loss (a person who dies), symbolic loss (a romantic breakup, for example) requires grief, and that implies a transition period between life with that person and a new life without them.

In the case of a romantic breakup, it is essential to understand that what you desire or need in a relationship cannot be found in that person, whether because they don't want to or can't give it to you. It doesn't matter if things were different in the past: the reality is that now you can no longer count on that person in a romantic sense. They can't or won't be your partner. Clinging to this will make both of you suffer unnecessarily.

To accept the separation, you must reflect on what that relationship brings you today or what it brought you during the time immediately before the breakup. Is this what you want or need for the rest of your life?

When a breakup is not accepted, the person often gets stuck in one of the first three stages of grief. Then, desires for revenge, stalking or controlling the other person's new life, refusing to move on, and trying to convince them may appear. None of this works.

When someone leaves your side, or when you decide to part ways with them, it is necessary to understand that you don't own anyone, and no one belongs to you as if they were an object you bought. While fidelity and commitment are part of emotional responsibility, believing that someone owes you their love is completely immature.

Grieving for those who hurt you

Constantly remembering those who hurt you not only causes unnecessary suffering in the present but also prevents you from healing.

This happens when you repeatedly ask yourself how that person could have hurt you so much, how they could have betrayed you that way, or how people can be so cruel. It also occurs when you plot revenge (which usually harms the plotter more than the target) or hold grudges (you can never be happy while living in resentment).

So, should you forgive those who hurt you intentionally?

In cases of injustice, many psychologists encourage victims to forgive. I don't share that opinion. Forgiving someone who didn't care about hurting you, who would do it again if they could, or who never showed or shows remorse is absurd and a humiliation for the victims. It's one thing not to live with a grudge, and another to forgive someone who laughs at your pain.

Forgiveness, in my opinion, can come naturally after recovery, and it is a personal choice for each victim. In my experience, it is possible to heal and overcome the wounds of betrayal and abandonment without actually forgiving the aggressor or abuser.

Instead, the key is to grieve properly. How do you approach grieving for someone who hurt you?

Grieving in this case is:

- For the trust you placed in that person and lost.

- For the time you dedicated to that person without them deserving it, which you will never get back.

- For all the time you spent trying to recover from the wounds and maintain the relationship simultaneously, while the other person didn't even seem concerned.

- For everything that could have been and wasn't because of that person or what they did to you.

- Because that person is "dead" in the sense that they can never again have your trust or admiration.

- Because that person never existed (the person you had idealized or thought was different).

- For the person you were then when they hurt you, and you couldn't defend yourself.

Once the grief is processed, you can let go. You will never forget, but you will be able to accept it as part of your history (and not as part of your present).

I conclude with a quote from Steve Maraboli that I find especially inspiring: "Letting go means to come to the realization that some people are a part of your history, but not a part of your destiny."

Summary of Chapter 5

- Grief is the process of adapting to a new reality after a loss.

- Grief is usually for the real loss (death) of a loved one, but it can also be for other circumstances, such as a romantic breakup, illness, or job loss.

- Grief typically requires five successive stages: denial, anger, bargaining, depression, and acceptance.

- Grief can be short or long, and that does not determine anything. What makes grief pathological is getting stuck in one of its phases.

- We must allow ourselves to grieve for everything we deem necessary.

Use strategies for letting go

"I demolish my bridges behind me – then there is no choice but forward."

— Fridtjof Nansen

There is no instruction manual or magic formula for letting go of someone or something without suffering. However, there are some strategies to make it more bearable.

In this chapter, we'll explore ten techniques that will help you in the process of letting go of attachments. If this book were a cookbook, these techniques would be like the different knives available.

Before we start, we need to accept something to avoid feeling like a failure from the get-go: letting go does NOT guarantee immediate happiness. You won't wake up tomorrow and say, "Wow, I've let go, now I'm happy. What a difference!". But what is certain is that if you don't let go, you will never be happy.

Strategy 1: Turn to your archives

You already know that an archive is a place where records of real events are kept in the form of news or current events to be available for consultation. Applied to our lives, we could say that the archive is where our past is stored.

And we've already said that the past is a place to consult and learn from (not to live in!), and that's what we'll do in this exercise:

1. Think of a dysfunctional attachment you have at the moment that you don't want to let go of out of fear of not knowing how to live without it or failing without it.

2. Once you've identified the attachment and confirmed that it still causes you distress, keep it in your mind. Remind yourself that this exercise is to demonstrate that you have the resources to move forward without it. You are ready, and nothing bad will happen.

3. Now, go to your archive to find past situations where you broke attachments you were very attached to: your training wheels when you were little, your brother when he moved abroad, your first partner, your best friend, your grandfather's advice...

4. Mentally recreate the process of letting go, whether it was voluntary on your part or a natural event that occurred. Ask yourself if you were able to survive then. Convince yourself that, just as you did then, you will now find a way to continue and grow without it.

The goal of this exercise is not to make you believe in magical revelations from your past but to convince you that you can let go, because you are capable of continuing without something.

Strategy 2: Zero contact

We call "zero contact" a conscious and voluntary decision to cut off all means of communication with a toxic person with whom we have had some type of relationship, especially a narcissistic person.

It's very tempting to look for that person online, ask others about them, or drop hints for them on social media. Don't do it; it's useless, and you'll only stay hooked.

Zero contact is also recommended for people who, while not toxic, still cause you pain today (for example, an ex-partner who has already moved on).

Not knowing anything about the other person makes it easier to avoid the temptation to "respond" with your actions and forces you to act according to your own criteria, not conditioned by how the other person might receive your actions.

To make a simple analogy, if you're an alcoholic in rehab, don't walk past your favorite bar or try to find out who's going there or if it's been renovated.

Strategy 3: Change of scenery

If you're trying to forget someone, don't go to places that remind you of them. If an accident or illness has kept you away from stages or ski slopes, don't visit them for a while. If you've decided to stop drinking, stay away from parties for now. Avoid unnecessary exposure.

Instead, try new things. Channel your energy into new projects or experiences. And I don't just mean signing up for painting classes "to do something new", because we already know you'll abandon them before the year is out. I mean doing some things differently or learning something that leads you to learn something new about yourself. If that something is painting classes, wonderful. But if not, don't do it just to fill your time with activities that mean nothing to you. Doing new things also means redecorating your house, learning to cook Greek food, adopting a puppy, watching series that don't interest you (yes, stepping out of your TV comfort zone), signing up for a masterclass on something you have no idea about or haven't been interested in until now, buying elegant shoes that are NOT your style, and more.

Of course, changing scenery also includes meeting new people. And new people can be your neighbor on the third floor with whom you've never exchanged more than two sentences. Ask her if she knows of a nearby gym or Italian restaurant – anything.

Strategy 4: Avoid those who add nothing

You should consider stopping tolerating people just because you feel bad about leaving them. You only have one life; don't let it be occupied by people who don't make you feel good. The less time you spend with toxic people, the more time you'll have to spend with people who are worth it.

Who are toxic people? It's easy: people who drain your energy! They include:

- Envious people.

- Dishonest people.

- Negative people.

- Perpetual victims or drama queens.

- Manipulative people.

- People with erratic behavior, where you never know if they are trustworthy or not.

- Gossipy and critical people.

- Defiant people.

We all have bad times and days when we are unbearable. You're not going to abandon a friend because he was a bit annoying one day. No one is perfect, and we must learn to tolerate. But there is a difference between being tolerant and being taken for a fool.

So, distance yourself from people who never add value to your life. If it's not possible to cut them off immediately because they are part of your family or workplace, you must learn to handle them (not manipulate them, these are different things) so they don't drain all your energy. Here are some strategies:

- Emotional distance: some of these people put on Oscar-worthy performances. Be impassive when you detect they're acting or, even if their suffering is real, insist that you're not obliged to help them.

- Limited information: don't offer sensitive or unnecessary information about yourself. Reduce interactions to neutral conversations and don't show your feelings on any subject that could become a weapon against you. Be vague, even forgetful, about things in your life. You'll be glad you did.

- Agree with them: "vampires" are often childish and spoiled people. Don't insist on changing them; they need to feel superior to you. Agree with them and move on.

- Limited time: try to always be too busy for these people. For one reason or another, the weeks fly by…and you can't find time for them.

Strategy 5: Care for yourself like someone else

Do you know the saying "advice is easy to give but hard to take"? Well, this strategy is about that.

The act of letting go is ultimately an act of self-love and self-respect. If you have low self-esteem, if you don't know how to respect yourself or set personal boundaries with certain people, you will always find excuses. So, let's transfer it to "another person".

Now, imagine your job is to help someone let go of a bond that is causing them a lot of pain and limitations. That person trusts you and puts themselves in your hands. It's your job, and you get paid for it. How would you do it?

Do this, but with yourself as the patient, and do it as professionally as possible. Don't play around; take it seriously, and if necessary, pay yourself a fee for this work.

Strategy 6: Practice giving up

This exercise is the strangest in the series. In fact, my friends can't believe I recommend it as therapy. But it works!

We've already talked about how we don't let go out of fear of facing life without that thing. And it's normal; your brain will always resist uncertain changes. But you know you can, and it's better for you, so show your brain that you will survive. How? With small daily tests to show it what you are capable of.

For example, change your pillow for one night. Instead of using your usual pillow, use another one for a night. Your brain will protest, of course.

But it's about showing your brain that you can overcome a "different" night. Or change sides of the bed if you always sleep on the same side. Or sleep on the couch one night for no reason.

Want more ideas? Eat standing up instead of sitting down. Don't watch TV or any online content for two days in a row. Drink your coffee without sugar. Listen to a song you don't like. Give up small things, and ask yourself the next day if it was "that bad".

The goal of this exercise is not to make your life miserable. It's to show your brain that you are capable of adapting to whatever comes your way.

Strategy 7: Focus your energy on the everyday

It's time to start focusing on your practical day-to-day actions and why you do them, from going to work to preparing dinner.

The idea is to go through a phase of "questioning" your present: what is your day-to-day like? Are you efficient in your tasks? Do you ever give thanks for what you have when you wake up each morning? Were you happy yesterday afternoon? What needed to happen that afternoon for your happiness to be complete?

By getting used to focusing on your present, you spend less energy thinking about, or overthinking, other things. You go step by step, being aware of your achievements. This way, you weaken self-sabotage, fear, and insecurity, and, above all, the enormous gravitational pull that your past exerts on you.

Strategy 8: Empty your house

This one is similar to Strategy 3 (change of scenery), but a little more radical: it's about physically cleaning your space to align it with the new phase you want to embark on.

So, in the style of Marie Kondo or minimalism[8], get rid of everything that doesn't serve you in your present moment: objects you don't use, photos, mementos, clothes you don't wear, books you haven't touched in years, papers, and so on.

If you're no longer with someone, remove any photos you have with them from your sight, or of the places or activities that remind you of them. If that person also betrayed you, destroy their photos.

Sell or give away any objects you don't use but still store. The tennis rackets from when you used to play, the guitar from when you dreamed of being a musician, the skis, the college clothes...Your home cannot hold more things from your past than from your present.

---

[8] Both Marie Kondo and the minimalist movement endorse getting rid of the huge quantities of things we accumulate in our houses and which bring us nothing on an emotional level.

From the past, keep only the objects that make you happy, that bring you peace, serenity, or gratifying memories. Remove from your horizon everything that harms you, even if it made sense in the past or if someone might feel offended. Analyze what surrounds you and apply the "add or remove" rule. Does this painting make you happy? Does it comfort you? Then keep it. Does it not mean anything to you, but it was a gift, and you feel bad throwing it away? Out. Is it a memento from adolescence, but it now causes you discomfort? Remove it from your sight. Does it not cause discomfort, but you don't even know why you have it? Get rid of it and make space for something new.

Also, get rid of all the "just in case" or "what if one day" items: give away the old brushes you keep in case you resume painting one day. Sell the surfboard that is still waiting for you to have time to surf again. Throw away the old piece of wood you're saving just in case. All of this will train you to let go of other emotional crutches and burdens.

Strategy 9: Think of the Zen cup

Do you remember the quote about the full cup at the beginning of Chapter 1? Here's the full story.

Legend has it that once, a very intelligent and wise man went to see a Buddhist monk because he still didn't have certain answers he longed to know.

To meet him, the man walked for days, climbed mountains, and generally went to great lengths because he really wanted to know the truth.

But when the monk greeted him, the visitor became nervous; he thought maybe he wasn't the person the monk expected to see, or perhaps he wasn't worthy of his answers. So he started talking to show that he was ready. The monk remained silent, waiting for the visitor to finish.

When they brought some tea, the man offered to pour it himself and kept talking.

Then, the monk took the teapot and kept filling the visitor's cup, even though it was already full. The tea overflowed the cup and started to spill onto the table.

Seeing this, the visitor stopped talking and pointed out that the cup was already full. The master stopped, but the tea had already spilled over the table and was dripping to the floor. When the man asked why he had done it, the master explained that, like the cup, the visitor was full of his own ideas and opinions, and hadn't set them aside to receive anything new. On the contrary, by trying to prove that he was ready or that he knew many things, he had prevented himself from receiving anything new.

Then, the man drank all the tea in his cup and offered the monk his empty cup to be filled.

This story illustrates what you miss out on when you don't allow anything new into your life. Remember, every time you free up space in your mind, your schedule, or your heart, you open the door for something good to happen and for life to surprise you.

Strategy 10: Farewell letter

Writing letters is a very common exercise in psychology for addressing various emotional issues. This particular exercise involves writing a farewell letter to the things you will no longer keep in your life. A final conversation (or monologue) about something.

I suggest you write your goodbye letter to something you will no longer allow to be in your life. The letter can contain references to people or things and can talk about the anger and resentment you've accumulated, the sadness and fear, or whatever else.

Here are some guidelines:

- In this letter, you should communicate everything that comes to mind (it's not a formal letter): everything you would have liked to do or say in that situation, all the things you regret about it, everything you would do now if you could go back, and so on.

- You should also make clear the reasons that led you to this decision (saying goodbye). Even if you didn't cause the event, the decision to end the subsequent discomfort is yours.

- You should end the letter by saying goodbye to that person, thing, or emotion with a commitment to yourself, a promise to take action.

- Imagine you have the person or situation in front of you. Read the letter to them. Read it as many times as necessary until you feel the letter liberates you, and that there's nothing more to say.

- Destroy the letter: Burn it or tear it up, take the ashes or pieces to a place far from your home, and bury them. Finish saying goodbye and leave.

Remember, even if the letter is addressed to a person, the idea is not for that person to read it at any time: this letter is just for you.

Summary of Chapter 6

- There are several strategies we can implement to deal with the process of letting go.

- Some physically symbolize the act of letting go, such as writing and burning a farewell letter or cleaning out past objects from your home.

- In other cases, zero contact with people who hurt us or who we need to forget is recommended.

- Changing our scenery, meeting new people, or focusing on our daily lives are actions we should never stop doing.

Prepare for the next day

"I own me, and therefore, I can engineer me."
— Virginia Satir

We have reached the final step in our process of letting go. This step is simple: it's about having the path ready before us so we don't get stuck once we've freed ourselves from our burdens.

I mentioned this already in Chapter 2: you need to have goals and projects that pull you forward, as the past can often pull you back.

When I say this, some patients often respond, "That's just kidding yourself! You want me to focus on fantasizing about the future so I don't look at the past." That's not the case. At least, not if you have followed my 7-step method. What I propose is having the next day prepared so that you don't fall back into past attachments. In other words, to avoid relapse.

To do this, your future goals, whether for next week or ten years from now, need to be inspiring. They should be purposes and projects you identify with, not dreams copied from others.

Why set new objectives?

The greatest doses of happiness you will receive in life come from the positive results of your own actions and decisions. For this, you need goals that inspire you to keep growing and acting according to your values.

Nathaniel Branden, a pioneer in the study of self-esteem, said that one of the fundamental pillars of a full life is living with purpose: that is, filling our lives with meaning. What does that mean? It means having projects aligned with your values, growth capacity, and passions.

Life purposes (also known as meanings or deep motivations) are the ultimate reasons why we want to live. They are personal and voluntary missions that tell us who we are and our place in the world. They are the things we would like to be remembered for in a hundred years.

These purposes guide your decisions and cannot be imposed by anyone. They don't need to be monumental or change the course of humanity: it's enough for them to make sense to you.

Do you know what your life purposes are? Do you know what you're living for today? Visualize yourself in a year. Picture yourself as an eighty-five-year-old who is happy with life. Why should you be happy? What have you achieved to put that satisfied smile on your face? A happy family? A useful and inspiring job for others? A significant discovery? Saving the family business? Building a new business with proud employees? Living a life of integrity despite the challenges you've faced?

We all have something we deeply desire. Something we enjoy doing or could do for hours. When we can, we make it pivotal in our lives. If we're a little less lucky, it accompanies us in our free time. If you want to be proud of yourself, if you want to go to bed each night with hope, find those goals.

Have a good plan

If you have goals, you must have plans. Plans are the roadmaps that will lead you to your goals.

What should a good plan include[9]?

---

[9] Dealt with in the books The Power of Goals (*www.danieljmartin.es/books/pog*) and The Power of Discipline (*www.danieljmartin.es/books/pod*).

1. What you've set out to improve or achieve in the form of specific goals (not just "grow spiritually", but specific targets).

2. Possible problems and their solutions. You can list them as you identify them.

3. Sacrifices: Things you'll need to give up during the plan or permanently.

4. Everything you're going to do in order to achieve them: new habits, dates, changes in spending dynamics, learnings, self-care improvements, and similar.

5. All the responses to the questions you can foresee right now.

Seek advice for your plan and ask experts for feedback. Many professionals offer consulting services and can help you.

Then, you should outline your plan in a series of steps. For example:

1. Define the goal. For example, changing cities or professional sectors.

2. Identify your strengths and virtues. What do you have working in your favor in relation to this goal?

3. Assess your current starting point. What are you lacking? List everything you need to achieve this goal in order of execution.

4. Set start and end dates. These can be approximate; you're not a fortune-teller.

5. When you begin, stay focused. Find a way to note achievements, progress, and failures.

Summary of Chapter 7

- In life, we always need goals and projects that excite and motivate us.

- These goals and projects can be big or small, significant for humanity or not; the important thing is that they are ours and make sense to us.

- Life goals and purposes should be accompanied by a realistic plan.

- Viewing the future with hope not only helps us let go, but also helps us know and love ourselves better.

Unchain yourself and take flight!

The process is complete. Here we part ways – for now. I hope you enjoyed this book and, more importantly, that you found the answers you were looking for.

From my perspective, I have emphasized the necessity of cutting ties with the past because it is essential for building the life we truly want.

As I've mentioned a few times in this book, the past and its attachments exert a powerful gravitational force on us. On one hand, this is beneficial, because they provide us with a sense of identity and belonging, which are essential for humans. On the other hand, we have seen how difficult it is to separate from things that once made sense, even though they may now be harmful. So, if you've made it this far, I can only congratulate you on committing to your own freedom. Not many people do, and believe me, there is no fulfillment without the ability to live according to who we are and not according to what is expected of us or what we did in the past. So, CONGRATULATIONS.

I hope I've helped you – even if it's just by taking the first step. In this guide, you've discovered a simple 7-step method to guide you through the process of letting go. And if, after reading this book, you stop fighting with your past – and with the person in the mirror from the moment you wake up until you go to bed – I will consider my mission accomplished.

Now you know that learning to let go leads to a life without fear of emptiness or uncertainty. Understanding that losses are a continuous and inevitable part of life, and facing them, is essential for inner wellbeing. Doing otherwise only leads to an endless emotional cycle.

It's your turn, now. I trust you haven't come this far just to stop here. I hope you continue to move forward and don't stop until you're sure that everything around you, all your attachments and bonds, add value to your life instead of subtracting it.

You cannot change the past, nor can you control what happens around you. But you can decide how you want it to affect you each day.

Go far, alone or in good company (there are no other options). Make sure to travel light, and don't be scared: you're ready to fly!

Daniel

Your opinion is very important

As I'm an independent author, your opinion is so important to me and to future readers like you. I would be hugely grateful if you would leave me **a review on your favorite store** to tell me what you thought of my book **so that I can keep on improving it**:

- What did you like best?
- Is there anything you felt was missing
- Who would you recommend it to?
- ...

A gift just for you!

Would you like to read **my next book totally FREE?** Scan the code below and **sign up to my readers' club**!

Great surprises await you there: be the first to read my new launches, listen to my audiobooks for free, get copies signed just for you…and much more!

Other books by Daniel J. Martin